At Shugakuin

Ken Arnold

a room for washing poems
the water's constant chatter

Washing Lines

A collection of poems

Ex Libris

LAUTUS PRESS

Also published by Lautus Press

Strings of Pearls: A collection of poems
Shorelines: A collection of poems
both selected by Janie Hextall and Barbara McNaught

This collection was first published 2011
This revised edition published 2015
Lautus Press, Ryton House, Lechlade, GL7 3AR

ISBN: 978-0-9568265-0-3

Designed and typeset in Minion Pro by Touchmedia, Cheltenham
Printed by Holywell Press, Oxford

A CIP catalogue record for this book is available from the British Library

Contents (poems added to this edition marked with *)

Illustrations

Washing Line

Joanna M Weston

clothes catch
on the branches
of the apple tree
    touch hems
    with pale blossom
and fray petals
that drift down
loosed by your white shirt
to make stars on grass.

I Stop Writing the Poem

Tess Gallagher

to fold the clothes. No matter who lives
or who dies, I'm still a woman.
I'll always have plenty to do.
I bring the arms of his shirt
together. Nothing can stop
our tenderness. I'll get back
to the poem. I'll get back to being
a woman. But for now
there's a shirt, a giant shirt
in my hands, and somewhere a small girl
standing next to her mother
watching to see how it's done.

War and Peace

Michael Longley

Achilles hunts down Hector like a sparrowhawk
Screeching after a horror-struck collared-dove
That flails just in front of her executioner, so
Hector strains under the walls of Troy to stay alive.
Past the windbent wild fig tree and the lookout
Post they both accelerate away from the town
Along a cart-track as far as double well-heads
That gush into the eddying Scamander, in one
Warm water steaming like smoke from a bonfire,
The other running cold as hailstones, snow water,
Handy for the laundry-cisterns carved out of stone
Where Trojan housewives and their pretty daughters
Used to rinse glistening clothes in the good old days,
On washdays before the Greek soldiers came to Troy.

Clearances 5

Seamus Heaney
In Memoriam M.K.H., 1911-1984

The cool that came off the sheets just off the line
Made me think the damp must still be in them
But when I took my corners of the linen
And pulled against her, first straight down the hem
And then diagonally, then flapped and shook
The fabric like a sail in a cross-wind,
They made a dried-out undulating thwack.
So we'd stretch and fold and end up hand to hand
For a split second as if nothing had happened
For nothing had that had not always happened
Beforehand, day by day, just touch and go,
Coming close again by holding back
In moves where I was x and she was o
Inscribed in sheets she'd sewn from ripped-out flour sacks.

A Warm Day

Louise Glück

Today the sun was shining
so my neighbour washed her nightdresses in the river –
she comes home with everything folded in a basket,
beaming, as though her life had just been
lengthened a decade. Cleanliness makes her happy –
it says you can begin again,
the old mistakes needn't hold you back.

A good neighbour – we leave each other
To our privacies. Just now,
She's singing to herself, pinning the damp wash to the line.

Little by little, days like this
will seem normal. But winter was hard:
the nights coming early, the dawns dark
with a gray, persistent rain – months of that,
and then the snow, like silence coming from the sky,
obliterating the trees and gardens.

Today, all that's past us.
The birds are back, chattering over seeds.
All the snow's melted; the fruit trees are covered with downy new
      growth,
A few couples even walk in the meadow; promising whatever they
      promise.

We stand in the sun and the sun heals us.
It doesn't rush away. It hangs above us, unmoving,
like an actor pleased with his welcome.

My neighbour's quiet a moment,
Staring at the mountain, listening to the birds.

So many garments, where did they come from?
And my neighbour's still out there,
fixing them to the line, as though the basket would never be empty –
It's still full, nothing is finished,
though the sun's beginning to move lower in the sky;
remember, it isn't summer yet, only the beginning of spring;
warmth hasn't taken hold yet, and the cold's returning –

She feels it, as though the last bit of linen had frozen in her hands.
She looks at her hands – how old they are. It's not the beginning,
                         it's the end.
And the adults, they're all dead now.
Only the children are left, alone, growing old.

Laundry

Ruth Moose

All our life
so much laundry;
each day's doing or not
comes clean,
flows off and away
to blend with other sins
of this world. Each day
begins in new skin,
blessed by the elements
charged to take us
out again to do or undo
what's been assigned.
From socks to shirts
the selves we shed
lift off the line
as if they own
a life apart
from the one we offer.
There is joy in clean laundry.
All is forgiven in water, sun
and air. We offer our day's deeds
to the blue-eyed sky, with soap and prayer,
our arms up, then lowered in supplication.

Women's Work

Gillian Clarke

Their books come with me, women writers,
their verses borne through the rooms
out between the plum trees to the field,
as an animal will gather things,
a brush, a bone, a shoe,
for comfort against darkness.

August Sunday morning,
and I'm casting for words,
wandering the garden sipping their poems,
leaving cups of them here and there in the grass
where the washing steams in the silence
after the hay-days and the birdsong months.

I am sixteen again, and it's summer,
and the sisters are singing, their habits gathered,
sleeves rolled for kitchen work,
rosy hands hoisting cauldrons of greens.
The laundry hisses with steam-irons
glossing the collars of our summer blouses.

Then quietly they go along the white gravel,
telling their beads in the walled garden
where *Albertine*'s heady rosaries spill
religious and erotic over the hot stones.
And there's restlessness in the summer air,
like this desire for poems,

our daily office.

Love Calls Us to the Things of This World

Richard Wilbur

The eyes open to a cry of pulleys,
And spirited from sleep, the astounded soul
Hangs for a moment bodiless and simple
As false dawn.
                    Outside the open window
The morning air is all awash with angels.

    Some are in bed-sheets, some are in blouses,
Some are in smocks: but truly there they are.
Now they are rising together in calm swells
Of halcyon feeling, filling whatever they wear
With the deep joy of their impersonal breathing;

    Now they are flying in place, conveying
The terrible speed of their omnipresence, moving
And staying like white water; and now of a sudden
They swoon down in so rapt a quiet
That nobody seems to be there.
                         The soul shrinks

    From all that it is about to remember,
From the punctual rape of every blessed day,
And cries,
               "Oh, let there be nothing on earth but laundry,
Nothing but rosy hands in the rising steam
And clear dances done in the sight of heaven."

Yet, as the sun acknowledges
With a warm look the world's hunks and colours,
The soul descends once more in bitter love
To accept the waking body, saying now
In a changed voice as the man yawns and rises,

"Bring them down from their ruddy gallows;
Let there be clean linen for the backs of thieves;
Let lovers go fresh and sweet to be undone,
And the heaviest nuns walk in a pure floating
Of dark habits,
                    keeping their difficult balance."

Sari

Imtiaz Dharker

The street stretches its back.
Its spine cracks with satisfaction.

There's no bustle, no sense of rush,
just the determined slip and slap
of soap on slate
and cloth on stone,
morning light thrashed out
on the wet step
above the water-tank.

Her arm an arc, her haunch
pushed back,
the whole length of sari
thwacked.
Legs apart, she attacks
the sweat of yesterday,
the cooling smells,
the dribble from the baby's mouth,
drives them out
of thin and daily thinning cloth.

Today she wears the purple,
washes green,
tosses it out to dry,
smacks it down across the stones
like an accomplishment
of fine clean weave.
Sun and light shine through.
Through and through,
the day begun.

The city rolls its hip,
picks up its plastic bucket,
walks away.

The Line

Maura Dooley

A heavy linen cloth,
her dress of shooting stars,
the brittle blue of spring,
his sodden woollen shirt.

The peg becomes a pen,
fills the line with cursive,
a changing word in wind,
love or *duty* or *life*.

A Reminder (Great Cranberry Island)

Carl Little

It is one sort of evidence of living:
      a wash hung in the yard
between the house and a tree or some such
      arrangement for holding things off
the ground. Sheets snap like sails,
      a bra trails a strap, its
guard let down. An only shirt (tropical
      fish pattern) flutters about
till its arms entangle or go limp for
      want of wind. What's dry

gets taken in before the dusk dampens it,
      the vacation over so to speak.
Once more a faded yellow towel will fold
      neatly in three or someone's
favourite pants be re-mended. Crisp linen
      may twist beneath lovers
excited to old desires by the freshness
      upon which they lie.
And as one supposes every household has

      its weakness, so each home
the length of this island has a wash.
      But of certain things
one must be, from time to time, reminded:
      happiness, for instance,
mortality, and even (and this is my argument)
      that wide assortment
of odd clothing that droops in the dark,
      forgotten tonight, haunting
the house to which we are all attached
      by a good strong cord

for William Kienbusch, 1914-1980

Dashing Away with the Smoothing Iron

Traditional

'Twas on a Monday morning
When I beheld my darling
She looked so neat and charming
In every high degree
She looked so neat and nimble, O
A-washing of her linen, O

Refrain
Dashing away with the smoothing iron
Dashing away with the smoothing iron
She stole my heart away.

'Twas on a Tuesday morning
When I beheld my darling
She looked so neat and charming
In every high degree
She looked so neat and nimble, O
A-hanging out her linen, *O (Refrain)*

'Twas on a Wednesday morning
When I beheld my darling
She looked so neat and charming
In every high degree
She looked so neat and nimble, O
A-starching of her linen, O *(Refrain)*

'Twas on a Thursday morning
When I beheld my darling
She looked so neat and charming
In every high degree
She looked so neat and nimble, O
A-ironing of her linen, O *(Refrain)*

'Twas on a Friday morning
When I beheld my darling
She looked so neat and charming
In every high degree
She looked so neat and nimble, O
A-folding of her linen, O *(Refrain)*

'Twas on a Saturday morning
When I beheld my darling
She looked so neat and charming
In every high degree
She looked so neat and nimble, O
A-airing of her linen, O *(Refrain)*

'Twas on a Sunday morning
When I beheld my darling
She looked so neat and charming
In every high degree
She looked so neat and nimble, O
A-wearing of her linen, O *(Refrain)*

Planet Earth

P K Page

> It has to be spread out, the skin of this planet,
> has to be ironed, the sea in its whiteness;
> and the hands keep on moving,
> smoothing the holy surfaces.

In Praise of Ironing by Pablo Neruda

It has to be loved the way a laundress loves her linens,
the way she moves her hands caressing the fine muslins
knowing their warp and woof,
like a lover coaxing, or a mother praising.
It has to be loved as if it were embroidered
with flowers and birds and two joined hearts upon it.
It has to be stretched and stroked.
It has to be celebrated.
O this great beloved world and all the creatures in it.
It has to be spread out, the skin of this planet.

The trees must be washed, and the grasses and mosses.
They have to be polished as if made of green brass.
The rivers and little streams with their hidden cresses
and pale-coloured pebbles
and their fool's gold
must be washed and starched or shined into brightness,
the sheets of lake water
smoothed with the hand
and the foam of the oceans pressed into neatness.
It has to be ironed, the sea in its whiteness.

and pleated and goffered, the flower-blue sea
the protean, wine-dark, grey, green, sea
with its metres of satin and bolts of brocade.
And sky – such an 0! overhead – night and day
must be burnished and rubbed
by hands that are loving
so the blue blazons forth
and the stars keep on shining
within and above
and the hands keep on moving.

It has to be made bright, the skin of this planet
till it shines in the sun like gold leaf.
Archangels then will attend to its metals
and polish the rods of its rain.
Seraphim will stop singing hosannas
to shower it with blessings and blisses and praises
and, newly in love,
we must draw it and paint it
our pencils and brushes and loving caresses
smoothing the holy surfaces.

Laundry

Gillian Clarke

Outside the shacks by the Tulsi Pipe Road
the women are laundering rainbows,
heaving cloth into tubs, load after load.
They lift and twist red, indigo, yellow
with their thin bangled arms,
as our foremothers might have done
in a mountain stream or tarn,
or a pure spring by the road.

They must wring every rag
for its strings of water-jewels,
to be saved and re-used.
They drape their glories like flags
over dipping wires and trees
dirtied at once in a lift of the breeze
by road-dust, particulates of petrol, diesel.
They will sleep dazed by the fumes.

Jerusalem

Yehuda Amichai (1924-2000)
Translated by Stephen Mitchell

On a roof in the Old City
Laundry hanging in the late afternoon sunlight:
The white sheet of a woman who is my enemy,
The towel of a man who is my enemy,
To wipe off the sweat of his brow.

In the sky of the Old City
A kite.
At the other end of the string,
A child
I can't see
Because of the wall.

We have put up many flags,
They have put up many flags.
To make us think that they're happy.
To make them think that we're happy.

In a Magdalene Laundry, County Cork, 1967

Kelly Morris

The air was so heavy-laden
with moisture, you could almost drink from it.
There was the chlorine of bleach, harsh
on the hands and sharp in the sinuses.
Blisters turned to calluses on hands
rubbed raw on washboards.
Did you know you can save your soul
if you scrub enough sheets?

Shapeless blue dresses hung from us
like shrouds and dark nuns floated
like ghosts with faces ironed flat.
This is what it must be like in Hell.
We're all sinners at heart,
Aren't we?

Mary's Wash Day

Dot McGinnis

On the flight into Egypt for all to see,
On an unscented shrub hung so tenderly,

Were the Christ Child's newly laundered clothes,
On a lavender bush, so the legend goes.

They had stopped to rest by the roadside there,
Mary's clean wet laundry was everywhere.

On this scentless shrub His clothes did lay,
Swaddling clothes, Mary's washday.

Though Herod's soldiers were all around,
The Holy Family could still be found,

Attending to the Christ Child's needs,
Along the wayside, among the weeds.

She hung them gently on this drying rack,
His swaddling clothes, a scent it did lack.

Still a symbol of virtue and purity,
"Our Lady's Shelter," so none could see.

It hid them while the soldiers passed,
So she gave it a blessing that would ever last.

A fragrance this shrub would no longer lack;
Spikenard, manger herb, drying rack.

For the bush that held the Christ Child's clothes,
Took on His scent and thus arose,

A smell so sweet beloved by Mary,
His precious scent it would always carry.

Thereafter, so the legend goes,
Lavender smelled of swaddling clothes.

Shirt

Jo Haslam

When I go outside in the autumn night
to fetch in washing that's almost dried
in the still mild air – and it's mostly my sons' T-shirts
and shirts, and they're mostly pale,
blue or white, I see how they hang
loose from the hem, how the empty sleeves
and cuffs just stir when I fill my arms
how they flop over the crook of my elbow
– and they're soft now and cool,
and I think how they'll open and swell
with the different shapes of my sons,
how even now those shapes are there
(how I can tell in the dark which shirt is which)
how they keep the scent of their flesh and sweat
under the astringent soapy smell; and when they're dressed
in those shirts and the cloth is close to the skin
how I can see their chests lift and depress,
the older son's narrow concave chest –
the way his ribs project – the younger
one taller and broader now. And I don't like to throw
a shirt away, even when it's worn so thin, the ribbed
side seams and welt have unstitched,
and it's rubbed so soft the dark blots of ink
and grease have washed in, become part of the cloth.
And I rub my fingers over the pearly nubs
Of buttons, over the frayed collar and cuffs,
then I take off the buttons and keep the rest
for shoe cloths and dust cloths. But before
I do with these shirts I bring in, that fall and flop
and wind themselves round and over my arms
the way my sons' real bodies don't anymore –

I slide a hand inside each one
as if I could find, like those Russian dolls
the smaller school shirts, sports shirts, T-shirts,
vests, the little cap sleeves and stretchy envelope necks,
the silky stitched hems; how it seems no more
from that time to this mild autumn, than it does from now
to the season ahead, when I'll go outside in the winter night
and prise off the line the same washed shirts
that are cold and white and stiff with frost.

Laundry

George Bilgere

My mother stands in this black
And white arrangement of shadows
In the sunny backyard of her marriage,
Struggling to pin the white ghosts
Of her family on the line.
I watch from my blanket on the grass
As my mother's blouses lift and billow,
Bursting with the day,
My father's white work shirts
Wave their empty sleeves at me,
And my own little shirts and pants
Flap and exult like flags
In the immaculate light.

It is mid-century, and the future lies
Just beyond the white borders
Of this snapshot; soon that wind
Will get the better of her
And her marriage. Soon the future
I live in will break
Through those borders and make
A photograph of her–but

For now the shirts and blouses
Are joyous with her in the yard
As she stands with a wooden clothespin
In her mouth, struggling to keep
The bed sheets from blowing away.

Spin-Cycle

Jane Holland

You've been blackberrying again.
I take your blouse
and watch it turn

through the white suds
in the drum, rinse-hold,
spinning slowly through the cycle.

I hear you up above,
bouncing on the bed
to reach the oval mirror,

see the purple stains
around your mouth and chin,
the blackness under nails

and in your hair.
Soon, like your swan-necked sister,
you will not have to stretch

on tip-toe for the sink
or grip the rail
when coming down the stairs.

You say 'when'.
I do not have the answers.
Just the slow loop

of your blouse
growing heavy with water,
as one cycle ends
and waits upon another.

Washing

Michael Longley

All the washing on the line adds up to me alone.
When the cows go home and the golden plover calls
I bring it in, but leave pegged out at intervals
Dooaghtry Lake and David's Lake and Corragaun,
Gaps in the dunes, a sky-space for the lapwings
And the invisible whiteness of your underthings.

The Lace-Maker

Gillian Clarke

A white farm, a black beach
and the long seas running.
At the click of the gate three gulls lift
from the sea and the wind sucks salt, fish
and cat-piss from the old lime kilns.

She comes between trees to fetch me home,
her apron full of pegs, her lace
cuffing the stones below the waterfall,
pearls beading the air, and in each hand
is one warm egg, laid wild.

Her sheets are out above the field,
tugging for Ireland in a westerly,
billowing slips for pillows and bolsters,
table cloths, petticoats,
angels in lace and clean linen.

She calls, shading her eyes from too much
sea-light, from straining too long, too often
by the wavering light of oil-lamps,
gas-light, a primitive electricity
too frail to stand those wild Atlantic winters,

when at the table she counted her stitches home
in a system of bobbins and beads till every tea
and bed-time were washed in the settled foam
of sea-flowers hooked in a detritus of bird-bones,
her knuckles ivoried with listening.

They That Wash on Monday

Traditional

They that wash on Monday
  Have all week to dry;

They that wash on Tuesday
  Are not much awry;

They that wash on Wednesday
  Are not so much to blame;

They that wash on Thursday
  Wash for shame;

They that wash on Friday
  Wash in need;

And they that wash
  On Saturday?

Dirty they are indeed!

Washing Day: Monday Morning 1966

Dawn Bauling

War is being done in the kitchen –
the grounding rounding up and downing
fight of sheet and shirt and pillowslip.
Steam scalds drip from spluttering taps,
trapped in the tropical clouds of Monday.
Reluctant sheets scream in the mangle,
tangle together, tribally twisting,
resisting, spitting their protests.
And the drum sounds, on and on,
slip slop slapping overweight towels,
beating vest and humbling underwear
with its rumbling, grumbling, tumbling
rhythm.
And strangled tights fight finally with socks
until the last one shrivelled-small and
pitiful,
is pincered from the waters' sucking,
drowning
grasp.

Then mother stands triumphant, hands
hipped,
par-boiled like a satisfied lobster,
bathed in aroma of hot cloth,
a proper washday Boudicca, examining her
spoils,
distilled dirt and simmered soil
glistening on her victorious face
while the waste, spitting loudly, disappears.

'Watch carefully, my girl,' I hear her say,
'this will be your job one day.'

But I would never be this glorious.

Washing-Day

Anna Laetitia Barbauld (1743-1825)

Come, Muse, and sing the dreaded *Washing-Day*.
–Ye who beneath the yoke of wedlock bend,
With bowed soul, full well ye ken the day
Which week, smooth sliding after week, brings on
Too soon; for to that day nor peace belongs
Nor comfort; ere the first grey streak of dawn,
The red-arm'd washers come and chase repose.
Nor pleasant smile, nor quaint device of mirth,
E'er visited that day: the very cat,
From the wet kitchen scared, and reeking hearth,
Visits the parlour, an unwonted guest.
The silent breakfast-meal is soon dispatch'd
Uninterrupted, save by anxious looks
Cast at the lowering sky, if sky should lower.
From that last evil, oh preserve us, heavens!
For should the skies pour down, adieu to all
Remains of quiet; then expect to hear
Of sad disasters – dirt and gravel stains
Hard to efface, and loaded lines at once
Snapped short – and linen-horse by dog thrown down,
And all the petty miseries of life.
Saints have been calm while stretched upon the rack,
And Guatimozin smil'd on burning coals;
But never yet did housewife notable
Greet with a smile a rainy washing-day.
– But grant the welkin fair, require not thou
Who call'st thyself perchance the master there,
Or study swept, or nicely dusted coat,
Or usual 'tendance; ask not, indiscreet,
Thy stockings mended, tho' the yawning rents

Gape wide as Erebus, nor hope to find
Some snug recess impervious: should'st thou try
The 'customed garden walks, thine eye shall rue
The budding fragrance of thy tender shrubs,
Myrtle or rose, all crushed beneath the weight
Of coarse check'd apron, with impatient hand
Twitch'd off when showers impend: or crossing lines
Shall mar thy musings, as the wet cold sheet
Flaps in thy face abrupt. Woe to the friend
Whose evil stars have urged him forth to claim
On such a day the hospitable rites;
Looks, blank at best, and stinted courtesy,
Shall he receive. Vainly he feeds his hopes
With dinner of roast chicken, savoury pie,
Or tart or pudding: – pudding he nor tart
That day shall eat; nor, tho' the husband try,
Mending what can't be help'd, to kindle mirth
From cheer deficient, shall his consort's brow
Clear up propitious; the unlucky guest
In silence dines and early slinks away.
I well remember, when a child, the awe
This day struck into me; for then the maids,
I scarce knew why, looked cross, and drove me from them;
Nor soft caress could I obtain, nor hope
Usual indulgencies; jelly or creams,
Relique of costly suppers, and set by
For me their petted one; or butter'd toast,
When butter was forbid; or thrilling tale
Of ghost, or witch, or murder – so I went
And shelter'd me beside the parlour fire:
There my dear grandmother, eldest of forms,
Tended the little ones, and watched from harm,
Anxiously fond, tho' oft her spectacles
With elfin cunning hid, and oft the pins

Drawn from her ravell'd stocking, might have sour'd
One less indulgent. –
At intervals my mother's voice was heard,
Urging dispatch; briskly the work went on,
All hands employed to wash, to rinse, to wring,
To fold, and starch, and clap, and iron, and plait.
Then would I sit me down, and ponder much
Why washings were. Sometimes thro' hollow bowl
Of pipe amused we blew, and sent aloft
The floating bubbles, little dreaming then
To see, Mongolfier, thy silken ball
Ride buoyant through the clouds – so near approach
The sports of children and the toils of men.
Earth, air, and sky, and ocean, hath its bubbles,
And verse is one of them – this most of all.

Wash Day

Jane Kenyon (1947-1995)

How it rained while you slept! Wakeful,
I wandered around feeling the sills,
followed closely by the dog and cat.
We conferred, and left a few windows
Open a crack.
              Now the morning is clear
and bright, the wooden clothespins
swollen after the wet night.

The monkshood has slipped its stakes
and the blue cloaks drag in the mud.
Even the daisies – good-hearted
simpletons – seem cast down.

We have reached and passed the zenith.
The irises, poppies, and peonies, and the old
shrub roses with their romantic names
and profound attars have gone by
like young men and women of promise
who end up living indifferent lives.

How is it that every object in this basket
got to be inside out? There must be
a trickster in the hamper, a backward,
unclean spirit.
              The clothes – the thicker
things – may not get dry by dusk.
The days are getting shorter...
You'll laugh, but I feel it –
Some power has gone from the sun.

I Wash the Shirt

Anna Swir

Translated from the Polish by Czeslaw Milosz and Leonard Nathan

For the last time I wash the shirt
of my father who died.
The shirt smells of sweat. I remember
that sweat from my childhood,
so many years
I washed his shirts and underwear.
I dried them
at an iron stove in the workshop,
he would put them on unironed.

From among all bodies in the world,
animal, human,
only one exuded that sweat.
I breathe it in
for the last time. Washing this shirt
I destroy it
forever.
Now
only paintings survive him
which smell of oils.

Ironing after Midnight

Marsha Truman Cooper

Your mother called it
"doing the pressing,"
and you know now
how right she was.
There is something urgent here.
Not even the hiss
under each button
or the yellow business
ground in at the neck
can make one instant
of this work seem unimportant.
You've been taught
to turn the pocket corners
and pick out the dark lint
that collects there.
You're tempted to leave it,
but the old lessons
go deeper than habits.
Everyone else is asleep.
The odour of sweat rises
when you do
under the armpits,
the owner's particular smell
you can never quite wash out.
You'll stay up.
You'll have your way,
the final stroke and sharpness
down the long sleeves,
a truly permanent edge.

A Song from the Suds

Louisa May Alcott (1832-1888)

Queen of my tub, I merrily sing,
While the white foam raises high,
And sturdily wash, and rinse, and wring,
And fasten the clothes to dry;
Then out in the free fresh air they swing,
Under the sunny sky.

I wish we could wash from our hearts and our souls
The stains of the week away,
And let water and air by their magic make
Ourselves as pure as they;
Then on earth there would be indeed
A glorious washing day!

Along the path of a useful life
Will heart's-ease ever bloom;
The busy mind has no time to think
Of sorrow, or care, or gloom;
And anxious thoughts may be swept away
As we busily wield a broom.

I am glad a task to me is given
To labour at day by day;
For it brings me health, and strength, and hope,
And I cheerfully learn to say –
"Head, you may think; heart, you may feel;
But hand, you shall work always!"

Windy Wash Day

Dorothy Aldis (1896-1966)

The wash is hanging on the line
And the wind's blowing –
Dresses all so clean and fine,
Beckoning
And bowing.

Stockings twisting in a dance,
Pyjamas very tripping,
And every little pair of pants
Upside down
And skipping.

Ironing

Vicki Feaver

I used to iron everything:
my iron flying over sheets and towels
like a sledge chased by wolves over snow;

the flex twisting and crinking
until the sheath frayed, exposing
wires like nerves. I stood like a horse

with a smoking hoof
inviting anyone who dared
to lie on my silver padded board,

to be pressed to the thinness
of dolls cut from paper.
I'd have commandeered a crane

if I could, got the welders at Jarrow
to heat me an iron the size of a tug
to flatten the house.

Then for years I ironed nothing.
I put the iron in a high cupboard.
I converted to crumpledness.

And now I iron again: shaking
dark spots of water onto wrinkled
silk, nosing into sleeves, round

buttons, breathing the sweet heated smell
hot metal draws from newly-washed
cloth, until my blouse dries

to a shining, creaseless blue,
an airy shape with room to push
my arms, breasts, lungs, heart into.

That Moment

Marie Kazalia

on the flat rooftop
in the hot dry tropical sky
me the only foreigner
white woman amid brown
as I try scrubbing
my pink lace Dior demi-cup
underwire bra
on the black granite
washing stone
chiselled with texture
to create a scrub board
surface slanted
laundry soap in a blue bar
bucket of cold water
Burning hot air – bright sun
looking down at my own hands
fumbling with my efforts
trying   yet stop
in amazement at the moment
stare into my mind
the ridiculous incongruities
in my life
Living ways that make no sense
to me or anyone else
Yet that moment of the most
powerful significance –
little Siva comes to my rescue
just eighteen   laughing at me
giving a lesson in how to wash
clothes in a bucket
on a washing stone in the heat
and poverty of inconvenience
South India –

Washing Clothes

Rati Saxena

They rub off every speck of dirt
From the collars of shirts, pockets and folds
Removing meaninglessness from every word

They rinse the clothes
One by one in the bucketful of water
Dipping every meaning in the work
They beat and rub and wash
In the flowing waters of meaning
Shake the clothes, smooth the folds,
And put them on the line
Decorating the word with the shell of meaning
Every dried cloth on the line is her poem
Washing clothes is not advertisement for soaps

(Trivendrum, Kerala, India)

Washerwomen at Würzburg

Michael Hulse

In cotton polka dot and check
the washerwomen work in line
on the scrubbed and scoured and barren deck
of a washboat on the Main.

Thick-ankled, heavy-hipped, they bend
To wash the daily dreck away.
Dirt of the living, world without end:
tomorrow is another day.

Thirty-nine or thereabouts,
the photograph. The river flows
as time requires. Whatever doubts
it washes with it no one knows.

Doing Laundry

Sandra Gilbert

I am doing laundry in my laundry room
the washing machine grinds and pumps like my father's heart
it is sick   it is well
sick again   well again

behind the round window your shirts
leap and praise God slowly like gentle souls
and my old brassieres bound like the clean breasts
of antelopes

I am doing laundry in Africa
and overhead the parrots shriek
they encourage me to beat harder
beat the dirt out of the flowers

I am doing laundry in Indiana
my husband the insurance salesman comes in
wanting to know if I would like to buy his new
insurance against laundry

I am doing laundry in the river Styx
I pound and I pound
the shirts disappear
the brassieres dissolve to nothingness

I am a heart doing laundry
and I beat and I pound
until I no longer remember
the colour of dirt

A Washing Machine Repairman Speaks on Poetry

Liz Gallagher

The repairman says that poetry is over-rated, meanwhile
he eases his shoulder against a jammed washing machine
door. There is no budging. The blanket inside is the exact

same colour as my cat. Tinges of brown and cream wool
swell out among dried-up bubbles behind the glass door.
The repairman says that this blanket could be ruined for life,

the way poetry ruins heads and sets highfaluting words into a spiral
motion that causes the world to fight on its side with a short sword.
Memories should be murky, he says. To clarify his point, he explains

the theory of gravitational pull. *If another planet joined the Moon,*
Earth would be doomed to be on the pull for umpteen days
and as many nights, where would that leave us? He doesn't wait

for an answer and my blanket is bursting to break glass.
We would be stuck in old Chevrolet cars, mincing hoots
and horns with our neighbours, making for the hills with half-open

suitcases and pet dogs trailing us. I look at my blanket;
it is pressed all squelched against the glass. The glass begins
to vibrate. The repairman keeps talking. *Well, that's what I mean*

about poetry, we don't need it snapping at our heels, asking us to look
back,
if a tidal wave is behind you, you just keep running. The vibrating gets
louder,
the door shoots off its handle, hitting my repairman in his third eye.
The blanket

heaves out, then flops in the sticky suds. A mini-wave in my own
kitchen

Mangles

Leontia Flynn

Washboards and mangles are on my father's mind.
In conversation he will return to the soaked linen
of his childhood – its labour-intensiveness –
as though these shirts and sheets, ready for the line,
floated behind my head in a basin together

and he could reach across and bring them in
amazed how they come up white again and again
after all these years – the marriage, the 'money-grubbing',
the house overrun by lunatic women
putting one thing after another through the wringer.

Washing Day in Dublin

Magi Gibson

You stoop, lift a sodden towel, pin it
to the drying rope. As in a silent dance,
you, your mother, bend, stretch, rise.

On your right, the fuschia bush
planted when you were a child
drips with red and purple buds.
High above clouds white and frothed as suds
scud across the blue sheet of the skies.

Once in this garden you ran wild,
once you dreamed below the bramley tree,
once you fought and played while Rosie
from the kitchen window watched and smiled.

No child upon it now, the old swing sways
an ancient creaking pendulum -
it ticks away the days since
you have swung from boy to man
who helps his mother hang the washing out

while from the kitchen window
another woman holds you in her gaze.

Pegging Out

Gillian Clarke

As she hangs out the clothes in the rising sun
in that wild space over trees and hedges,
bed-linen billowing, putting to sea,
his shirt-arms aloft, the dawn full of gestures
as when he dressed in the morning,

she listens to the collared dove complain
from the plum tree. It occurs to her that the bird
sings to the score of the wavering blurred
illegible longhand of a high slow plane
murmuring, fly away, fly away,

over and over the same three syllables
to the beat of ripe fruit falling in the grass.

Domestic

Katrina Porteous

My knuckles ache to pin them down,
Fresh as they smell. White clouds stream whipstruck
Over the chimneys. In the yard
The loud washing cracks on the line.

They strain to be off, the sheets and socks
I've washed for them these seven years:
Shirts like sails and the kids' wild colours,
Safe, familiar ironing:

They fling themselves before the wind.
Barely a few pegs hold them back.

Folding sheets

Marge Piercy

They must be clean.
There ought to be two of you
to talk as you work, your
eyes and hands meeting.
They can be crisp, a little rough
and fragrant from the line;
or hot from the dryer
as from an oven. A silver
grey kitten with amber
eyes to dart among
the sheets and wrestle and leap out
helps. But mostly pleasure
lies in the clean linen
slapping into shape.
Whenever I fold a fitted sheet
making the moves that are like
closing doors, I feel my mother.
The smell of clean laundry is hers.

Heaven on Earth

Craig Raine

Now that it is night,
you fetch in the washing
from outer space,

from the frozen garden
filmed like a kidney,
with a ghost in your mouth,

and everything you hold,
two floating shirts, a sheet,
ignores the law of gravity.

Only this morning,
the wren at her millinery,
making a baby's soft bonnet,

as we stopped by the spring,
watching the water
well up in the grass,

as if the world were teething.
It was heaven on earth
and it was only the morning.

Ode to Ironing

Pablo Neruda (1904-1973)
Translated by Jodey Bateman

Poetry is white
it comes dripping out of the water
it gets wrinkled and piles up
We have to stretch out the skin of this planet
We have to iron the sea in its whiteness
The hands go on and on
and so things are made
the hands make the world every day
fire unites with steel
linen, canvas and calico come back
from combat in the laundry
and from the light a dove is born
purity comes back from the soap suds.

The Washerwoman Beats the Laundry

Fernando Pessoa (1888-1935)
Translated by Richard Zenith

The washerwoman beats the laundry
Against the stone in the tank.
She sings because she sings and is sad
For she sings because she exists:
Thus she is also happy.

If I could do in verses
What she does with laundry,
Perhaps I would lose
My surfeit of fates.

Ah, the tremendous unity
Of beating laundry in reality,
Singing songs in whole or in part
Without any thought or reason!
But who will wash my heart?

Anna on the Beach

Dyea, Alaska, October 1897

Broken crates rim the leeshore like driftwood.
Men scramble, clumsy as crabs, to rescue
their outfits from the coming tide. Where Abe stood
minutes before, a man – sunk in his boots –
clings to a tipped platform: his year's ration
(sacks of flour, dried soup, lard) skims atop
the undertow. On shore: Anna, washing,
whittling lye soap into melted ice, chopped
from the stream bank. Abe haggles with packers
over price per pound. From a man, beaten
and bound for home, he buys an old pack-horse.
Anna hangs pants on tent lines to freeze them
stiff and dry. She loads her washing machine:
ten thousand men – just me to keep them clean –

Anna at the Washboard

She stretches the shirt to its full yardage,
scrubs the double seams of each sleeve and cuff
across the washboard's hollow rib cage
until the mud stains lift and lighten enough
to whiten in a load of lye and blue.
She turns the crank, but Abe's voice still echoes:
divining the map to their sure fortune,
reciting the code of each tool he chose
from a guidebook of goods to order by mail,
mouthing their new names, like Adam reborn –
compass, rock hammer, pickaxe, gold pan, scale.
But Anna refused the language he learned,
his spurned English, that gibberish of hope.
She chose a washer and three months of soap.

Taken from *Anna, washing* by **Ted Genoways**, an anthology of poetry set in Alaska telling the
story of two immigrants, Anna and Abe Malm. Abe is consumed by the romance of gold dust
while Anna sets up a laundry business in an effort to impose order through cleanliness.

The Odyssey (Book 6)

Homer
Translated by Robert Fitzgerald (1910-1985)

Nausikaa took the reins and raised her whip,
lashing the mules. What jingling! What a clatter!
But off they went in a ground-covering trot,
with princess, maids, and laundry drawn behind.
By the lower river where the wagon came
were washing pools, with water all year flowing
in limpid spillways that no grime withstood.
The girls unhitched the mules, and sent them down
along the eddying stream to crop sweet grass.
Then sliding out the cart's tail-board, they took
armloads of clothing to the dusky water,
and trod them in the pits, making a race of it.
All being drubbed, all blemish rinsed away,
they spread them, piece by piece, along the beach
whose pebbles had been laundered by the sea;
then took a dip themselves, and, all anointed
with golden oil, ate lunch beside the river
while the bright burning sun dried out their linen.
Princess and maids delighted in that feast;
then, putting off their veils,
they ran and passed a ball to a rhythmic beat,
Nausikaa flashing first with her white arms.

Parsley Sage Rosemary and Thyme

Traditional

Can you make me a cambric shirt,
   Parsley, sage, rosemary, and thyme,
Without any seam or needlework?
   And you shall be a true lover of mine.

Can you wash it in yonder well,
   Parsley, sage, rosemary, and thyme,
Where never sprung water, nor rain ever fell?
   And you shall be a true lover of mine.

Can you dry it on yonder thorn,
   Parsley, sage, rosemary, and thyme,
Which never bore blossom since Adam was born?
   And you shall be a true lover of mine.

Now you've asked me questions three,
   Parsley, sage, rosemary, and thyme,
I hope you'll answer as many for me,
   And you shall be a true lover of mine.

Can you find me an acre of land,
   Parsley, sage, rosemary, and thyme,
Between the salt water and the sea sand?
   And you shall be a true lover of mine.

Can you plough it with a ram's horn,
   Parsley, sage, rosemary, and thyme,
And sow it all over with one pepper-corn?
   And you shall be a true lover of mine.

Can you reap it with a sickle of leather,
  Parsley, sage, rosemary, and thyme,
And bind it up with a peacock's feather?
  And you shall be a true lover of mine.

When you have done and finished your work,
  Parsley, sage, rosemary, and thyme,
Then come to me for your cambric shirt,
  And you shall be a true lover of mine.

Clothesline Deceit

Marilyn K Walker

Miss Polly was a spinster
who lived a sheltered life
until a former classmate
asked her to be his wife.

But after they were married
she realized he was lewd.
It truly shocked Miss Polly
to know that he slept nude.

She wondered if her neighbours
observed her husband's ways
and noticed no pyjamas
were hung on laundry days.

Miss Polly went out shopping
and had a plan in mind!
She'd buy some men's pyjamas-
the brightest she could find.

Now when she meets her neighbours
she holds her head up high
just knowing those pyjamas
hang on her line to dry.

The Captainess of Laundry

Helen Dunmore

I am the captainess of laundry
and I sing to its brave tune,
to the crack and the whip and the flap of the sheets
and the rack going up, going down, going down
and the rack going up and going down,

I am the captainess of laundry
and I salt my speech with a song
of the bleach and the blue and the colours holding true
and the glaze of the starch on my skin, my skin,
and the glaze of starch on my skin,

I am the captainess of laundry
and I swing my basket through the town
with the sheets and the shirts and the white petticoats
and a snowy-breasted cover tied around, tied around
and a snowy-breasted cover tied around.

Enola Gay

Esther Morgan

She could be anybody's mother
pegging out the washing on a hot August morning,
lifting a sheet's saintly dazzle to the line.

The day stretches in front of her stainlessly:
her hands keep her busy, fluttering through each room
until all the windows are blinding.

She irons away the long afternoon,
pressing summer dresses thin as her own skin,
her face blurred by the clouds of steam.

Evening and his bedtime comes around again –
she used to kiss him, then tell him
to *Blow out the light!*

She crosses herself before falling asleep –
all night she flies for mile after starless mile
over fields of white linen.

Enola Gay
This Boeing B-29 Superfortress bomber became the first aircraft to
drop an atomic bomb as a weapon of war when, on 6 August 1945,
it targeted the city of Hiroshima, Japan. The plane was named after
Enola Gay Tibbets, mother of Paul Tibbets, the mission's pilot.

Six Bells

for the forty-four miners killed in the explosion on 28 June 1960
Gillian Clarke

Perhaps a woman hanging out the wash
paused, hearing something, a sudden hush,

a pulse inside the earth like a blow to the heart,
holding in her arms the wet weight

of her wedding sheets, his shirts. Perhaps
heads lifted from the work of scrubbing steps,

hands stilled from wringing rainbows onto slate,
while below the town, deep in the pit

a rock-fall struck a spark from steel, and fired
the void, punched through the mine a fist

of blazing firedamp. As they died,
perhaps a silence, before sirens cried,

before the people gathered in the street,
before she'd finished hanging out her sheets.

Ironing

Olivia McCannon

You've just shaved and you smell of cream.
I'm watching you press the metal point
Between buttons, over a collar, into a seam.

When you've left, I open the wardrobe quietly –
I want to climb in and hang there with your shirts
With my creases, waiting for you to iron them out.

Wood on cloth on cord

Amy Benedict

If I'm to be caught in a wave of terror
My whole sky life, wiped out
Blown to a tiny, dirt speck end
Vaporized into my next life
Without the long goodbye
The eye to eye pull kiss ending

Then catch me hanging sheets out in the sun

Out in the yard with the worms in the dark
Beneath the green, beneath my feet
With the sounds of this small city murmuring around me
The smell of clean, of apple, of breathing earth
The memory of love pressing, sighing, sobbing
Airing out the rhythm of rising and falling
Of giving in and letting go
And rising again

Finding just one edge to secure
Wood on cloth on cord
Forming a waving wall, a flag, a sail
Catch me hanging sheets out in the sun
Exposed, unveiled and holy
Undone

Washing on the Line

Borben Vladović translated by Miloš Đurđević

Backyards of the poor by the railway
  were cut by
washing lines with clothes drying.
Women's wet hearts were drying
and the frozen legs of trousers.
Train carriages were
making a noise and in their reflecting windows
clothes were fluttering and travelling
instead of their owners.
  Passengers
get their eyes, hands, ears,
mouths covered, but not their noses
so they can smell their destination
piled with neat clothes.

Arrival 1946

Moniza Alvi

The boat docked in at Liverpool.
From the train Tariq stared
at an unbroken line of washing
from the North West to Euston.

These are strange people, he thought –
an Empire, and all this washing,
the underwear, the Englishman's garden.
It was Monday, and very sharp.

Song of Myself

Walt Whitman (1819-1892)

Taken from stanza 3

I am satisfied – I see, dance, laugh, sing;
As the hugging and loving bed-fellow sleeps at my side through the night,
and withdraws at the peep of the day with stealthy tread,
Leaving me baskets cover'd with white towels swelling the house with their plenty...

Woman in a New House

Hugo Williams

First morning after our first night here,
Our bedroom full of dusty sunlight,
Whine of a sawmill next door, a radio
In the gardens and the noise of break
From the school in the field.

I am taking things out of old teachests
And packing them away in others. Am I
mad? I can throw them where I like!
My mind is crammed with love and ambition.
The future makes me fall asleep.

The basket I carried the washing in
Was an old wood basket from my father's house.
I found a washing line in the garden
And all my things flapping in the wind
With whip noises. I own the place.

Woman at Clothes Line

Anita Lahey

Strapped sandals lift the lady
above the lawn. Hung linens adopt her
hippy contours. This is no steamy

Tide commercial. Our star is absorbed
in cooler, wetter realities. She wears
a blue dress, white scarf. Her mouth

twitches wryly into some future. What
rustles toward her through the October
yard? Consider recklessness, how it breeds

in safe places. Was laundry ever just
a chore? Hold a rinsed blouse to your
face. Gaze through its weave at the gauzy

world. Notice how whiteness drinks itself
blue, agitates the fallen red
leaves. Those blankets have been under

your skin; they have things to tell you–
grey, woolly things. She lugs them out
to air their moth-eaten souls. How

gracefully she hoists her basket, all her
disappointments. It's clear from her eyes, the absence
of pins. Nothing here will blow away.

The Clothes Shrine

Seamus Heaney

It was a whole new sweetness
In the early days to find
Light white muslin blouses
On a see-through nylon line
Drip-drying in the bathroom
Or a nylon slip in the shine
Of its own electricity –
As if St Brigid once more
Had rigged up a ray of sun
Like the one she'd strung on air
To dry her own cloak on
(Hard-pressed Brigid, so
Unstoppably on the go) –
The damp and slump and unfair
Drag of the workaday
Made light of and got through
As usual, brilliantly.

Wash

Jane Kenyon (1947-1995)

All day the blanket snapped and swelled
on the line, roused by a hot spring wind...
From there it witnesses the first sparrow,
early flies lifting their sticky feet,
and a green haze on the south-sloping hills.
Clouds rose over the mountain... At dusk
I took the blanket in, and we slept,
restless, under its fragrant weight.

A Few Last Lines of Laundry

Eamon Grennan

This ragged shining,
these embodied nothings
are the image of us:

full of ourselves
in every puff of air
and hanging on

for dear life. At mid-day,
when the wind picks up,
such dancing. Look at us:

washed and stretched
to the very limit,
almost touching one another.

Acknowledgements

We would like to thank Neil Morgan and Jon Buckingham for their help and support in publishing this collection.

We would also like to thank the following poets and translators for permission to publish their poems:
Jodey Bateman, Dawn Bauling, George Bilgere, Miloš Đurđević, Magi Gibson, Jane Holland, Michael Hulse, Marie Kazalia, Dot McGinnis, Kelly Morris, Craig Raine, Rati Saxena, Borben Vladović and Jo Walton.

We gratefully acknowledge permission to reprint copyright material in this book as follows:
Arrival from *Split World: Poems 1990-2005* by Moniza Alvi (Bloodaxe Books 2005); *Jerusalem* from *The Selected Poetry of Yehuda Amichai* by Yehuda Amichai, edited and translated by Chana Bloch and Stephen Mitchell © 1996 (University of California Press); *At Shugakuin* from *Circle of the Way* by Ken Arnold, KenArnoldBooks, 2008 reprinted by permission; *The Lace-Maker, Laundry, Pegging Out, Six Bells* and *Women's Work* by Gillian Clarke (Carcanet); *Ironing after Midnight* by Marsha Truman Cooper originally published in *River Styx, No 32* 1990, selected for reprint as part of American Life in Poetry series, Ted Kooser (editor); *Sari* from *The Terrorist at My Table* by Imtiaz Dharker (Bloodaxe Books 2006); *The Line* from *Sound Barrier: Poems 1982-2002* by Maura Dooley (Bloodaxe Books 2002); *The Captainess of Laundry* from *The Malarkey* by Helen Dunmore (Bloodaxe Books 2012); *Ironing* from *The Handless Maiden* by Vicky Feaver (Jonathan Cape reprinted by permission of the Random House Group Ltd); *Mangles* from *These Days* by Leontia Flynn (Jonathan Cape reprinted by permission of the Random House Group Ltd); *A Washing Machine Repairman Speaks on Poetry* by Liz Gallagher from her collection; *I Stop Writing the Poem* from *Moon Crossing the Bridge* copyright © 1992 by Tess Gallagher, reprinted with the permission of Graywolf Press, Minneapolis, Minnesota, www.graywolfpress.org; *Anna on the Beach* and *Anna at the Washboard* from *Anna, Washing* by Ted Genoways, © 2008 by Ted Genoways, reprinted by permission of the University of Georgia Press; *Doing Laundry* by Sandra Gilbert (from *In the Fourth World*, University of Alabama Press 1979, republished in *Kissing the Bread: New and Selected Poems 1969-1999* W W Norton & Co 2000); *A Few Last Lines of Laundry* by Eamonn Grennan from *The Poetry Anthology (1912-2002)* edited by Joseph Parisi and Stephen Young, Ivan R Dee Inc (2002); *A Warm Day* from *Village Life* by Louise Glück (Carcanet); *Shirt* from *The Sign for Water* by Jo Haslam (Smith/ Doorstep Books 1998); *In Memoriam* from *Opened Ground: Poems 1966-1996* by Seamus Heaney © 1998 by Seamus Heaney and *The Clothes Shrine* from *Electric Light* by Seamus Heaney © 2001 by Seamus Heaney (Faber & Faber Ltd); Excerpt from Book 6 The Odyssey by Homer, trans by Robert Fitzgerald, copyright © 1961, 1963 by Robert Fitzgerald, renewed 1989 by Benedict R C Fitzgerald on behalf of the Fitzgerald children, reprinted by permission of Farrar, Straus & Giroux LLC; *Wash* and *Wash Day* by Jane Kenyon from *Collected Poems*, © 2005 by The Estate of Jane Kenyon, reprinted with the permission of Graywolf Press, Minneapolis, Minnesota, www.graywolfpress.org; *Woman at Clothes Line* from *Out to Dry in Cape Breton* by Anita Lahey, © Anita Lahey 2006, used by permission of the author and Signal Editions, Véhicule Press; *A Reminder (Great Cranberry Island)* from *Ocean Drinker* by Carl Little (Deerbrook Editions 2006); *War and Peace* and *Washing* from *Collected Poems* by Michael Longley (Jonathan Cape reprinted by permission of the Random House Group Ltd); *Ironing* from *Exactly My Own Length* by Olivia McCannon (Carcanet); *Laundry* from *Making the Bed* by Ruth Moose (Main Street Rag Press 2004); *Enola Gay* from *Grace* by Esther Morgan (Bloodaxe Books 2011); *Planet Earth* reprinted from *Planet Earth* by P.K. Page by permission of The Porcupine's Quill, copyright © the Estate of P.K. Page, 2002; *The Washerwoman Beats the Laundry* by Fernando Pessoa translated by Richard Zenith reprinted by permission of SLL/Sterling Lord Literistic, Inc, © by Richard Zenith; *Folding sheets* from *My Mother's Body* by Marge Piercy, copyright © 1985 by Marge Piercy and Middlemarsh Inc. Used by permission of the Wallace Literary Agency Inc (UK); *Domestic* from *The Lost Music* by Katrina Porteous (Bloodaxe Books 1996); *I Wash the Shirt* by Anna Swir translated by Czeslaw Milosz and Leonard Nathan from *Talking to my Body* English translation copyright © 1996 by Czeslaw Milosz and Leonard Nathan, reprinted with the permission of Copper Canyon Press www.coppercanyonpress.org; *Washing Line* by Joanna M Weston, originally published in Weyfarers 98; *Love Calls Us to the Things of This World* from *Things of This World*, copyright © 1956 and renewed 1984 by Richard Wilbur, reprinted by permission of Faber & Faber Ltd; *Woman in a New House* from *Collected Poems* by Hugo Williams (Faber & Faber Ltd)

We would also like to thank the following artists for their generous permission to reproduce their work in this book:
Clifford Harper (agraphia.co.uk), Anne Hayward, Beth Krommes, David Roland Leighton, artistic and literary executor to the estate of Clare Leighton (1899-1989), Miriam Macgregor, Pam Pebworth, Oscar Pletsch, Elizabeth Rashley, Sue Scullard (*Vegetable Garden at Lark Rise* © Sue Scullard for the Folio Society edition of *Lark Rise to Candleford*), Daniel Waters (www.indianhillpress.com), Sarah Young (www.sarahyoung.co.uk)

Every effort has been made to trace or contact all copyright holders. The publishers would be pleased to rectify any omissions brought to their notice at the earliest opportunity.

Doing laundry on the last day of the world

Jo Walton

Even if we never wear these shirts,
lie on these sheets,
eat off these tablecloths,
they will still flap out blue
between the buildings,
an unexpected line of colour
like a grace note.
(And should we live to bring them in
they will smell like fresh sunshine.)

Happiness lies poised between
eternity
and the next moment.
This shirt reaching out its wet arms
to yesterday's wind and sun,
now dryly embraces my arms.
And every leek cut lengthways,
every garlic clove chopped,
every basil leaf
is both its own good
and the potential of a meal
if the world goes on so long.

Yes, we could die on any morning,
slipping between moments,
gone between words in a conversation,
our worlds could end at any time.
Yet here we are, doing laundry,
making dinner,
making poetry,
making the mindful choices,
living in every moment,
because it is this moment,
every action its own action,
every word a benison.